FUNNY IS FUNNY

VOLUME 1

By: Joseph Senese

Copyright © 2019 Joseph Senese

All rights reserved.

ISBN: 9781693603068

DEDICATION

**To my parents: Rose & Mike Senese.
Thank you for teaching me that funny is funny.**

Do **NOT** buy this book if:

You are easily offended.

You are devoutly religious.

You are sensitive to foul language.

You value high moral standards.

You take yourself too seriously.

You are not sarcastically inclined.

You cannot tolerate anything out of your comfort zone.

You have a limited sense of humor.

You abhor rudeness and all the synonyms associated with it.

You have recently suffered from butt-hurt.

You are in search of a reading experience that is similar to the Bible.

<u>Buy</u> this book if:

You have been described as being slightly off-center.

You don't mind unleashing your subconscious for play-time.

You need to purchase an inexpensive gift for someone who shares your madness.

You welcome inappropriate thoughts.

You forgot what it's like to lighten up, unwind, and smile while you read.

You wish to appear slightly naughty and edgy to your peers.

You enjoy laughing at the expense of others.

You want to challenge your common sense.

You believe that you are not alone with your psychosis.

You can't remember the last time you laughed out loud.

You subscribe to the rule that *FUNNY IS FUNNY*.

"When you're finished reading this book, the best endorsement you can give is to tell your family and friends that it made you laugh, it made you think, and you enjoyed it so much, you could've eaten the ass out of it.

-joseph senese

You know that you've reached a certain stage in life, when you climb into the shower and have to grasp on to the bathroom wall for safety like you're attempting to scale Mount fucking Everest.

As a greeting to a friend, men sometimes put the word "Big" in front of their names. Examples of this are: "Hi, Big Jim." "Is that a new car, Big Steve?" "How's work, Big Lou?" Why don't women do this?
Examples: "Fancy seeing you here, Big Cindy." "That's a beautiful coat, Big Karen." "I love your hairdo, Big Shirley!"

If you win lots of money in the lottery, share it with as many people as you can. (Just the news that you've won, NOT the money.)

There's no place like home…unless you are homeless.

If you have friends in both low and high places, that makes you an extremely formidable foe. You are automatically a member of the "Don't Fuck With Club."

If you are experiencing déjà vu, you were probably as much of an asshole then, as you are now.

Do dwarfs that perform oral sex on a taller partner refer to it as "going up" on them?

When you share your problems with friends, and they tell you not to worry, what they mean is that they have no interest in hearing about your fucking problems.

Advice for Storm Chasers:

Stop chasing storms, and get up close and personal with those nasty bitches! You safely park three miles away in your rusted van with that crooked antennae that precariously dangles off the roof. Then, you have the balls to take video footage, by pointing that five-year-old camera with the 10-inch telescopic lens (which you probably maxed out your credit card to purchase at a pawn shop), out of that filthy, cracked windshield with the broken wiper blade that's stuck in the "up" position. The interior of that shit-box you refer to as your 'chase vehicle,' is littered with cheap fast-food wrappers, and smells like a putrid combination of old urine stored in plastic jugs, farts, body odor, and cigarette smoke. So, the next time you go chasing a storm, get your lazy ass outside and run directly into that fucking tornado, you big pussy.

You know that you're drunk when you open your refrigerator and proceed to urinate inside the fruits and vegetable drawer.

Is it acceptable to tell a prospective Native American job candidate that you have some reservations about hiring them?

Most women usually agree that a way to a man's heart is through his stomach unless that man is a Vegan. Then, the only way to his heart would be through his vagina.

When a man flashes lots of money, it means one of two things, either he has a lot of money, or he has a small dick. (You're on your own to figure out which one it is.)

When someone starts a conversation with you by saying, "I hate to be the bearer of bad news," remind them that you're carrying a gun.

When life gives you lemons, make lemonade, an apple a day keeps the doctor away, asparagus makes your urine smell, broccoli and cauliflower give you gas. What is the resolve to the evils of these fruits and vegetables? Eat a fucking steak.

While masturbating, always remember that if you die before having an orgasm, whoever finds you will probably know what you were doing. If they are not listed as a beneficiary in your will, they'll sure as shit share that information (including pictures) on social media.

Money can't buy happiness. This is the biggest lie in history.

Calling your parents to see how they're doing is a very loving gesture unless they're both dead.

If someone says, "I feel like I've met you in another life," answer them by saying, "I feel the same way." Then, remind them that they still owe you $300.

You know that you're self-centered when a family member or friend dies, and all that you can think about is how much you'll be inconvenienced by attending their wake or funeral.

Shit will always taste like shit, no matter what topping you sprinkle on it.

Atheists do not believe in God. Worshiping an entity is not for them, but what are their thoughts about hell? That is a place, and by all accounts; it doesn't sound like a vacation destination. So, here's wishing all of you Atheists the very best with eternal damnation, pain, suffering, and having your genitals engulfed in flames for all of eternity. (We would pray for you, but we know that you wouldn't want us to waste our time.)

Don't confuse an inactive brain with an underactive thyroid.

Do Italian men wear gold chains so they know when to stop shaving?

If something is needless to say, why bother to say it?

If you are forced to share your opinion on something, make sure it is socially unacceptable, vile, and repulsive. You'll never have to worry about being asked to share it again.

Beg, borrow and steal to get what you want. You'll get it quicker and easier than working for it.

If you don't fear the rain, but only where it comes from, you are afraid of clouds. You are a fucking imbecile.

Ugly people are fully aware that they are ugly. If they pretend that they're not, they are also liars.

If you are your own worst enemy, and your enemy's enemy is your friend, you have just made a friend for life. Well done.

In today's job culture, if you whistle while you work, your boss will probably write you up. If you are a member of a labor union, you can file a grievance. That's an awful lot of shit to deal with for just whistling. You're much better off sneaking an alcoholic beverage, or smoking a joint on your breaks and lunch hour. #madeinAmerica.

If someone offers you unsolicited advice, kindly listen to what they have to say. When they are done, thank them for their concern. Later, preferably in the middle of the night, call them up on the phone screaming hysterically to mind their own fucking business and then hang up on them.

Were there any conspiracy theories when Jesus was killed?

If someone you haven't seen for a while greets you, and then rudely follows it by saying that it looks like you've aged, gained weight or are losing your hair, respond to them by asking how their recently deceased spouse, parent, or child are doing.

Seeing is believing does not apply to the blind, they will just have to take your word for it.

Breakfast is not the most important meal of the day, dinner is. If you choose to have breakfast food for dinner, you're probably just broke until payday.

There is nothing better than sex in the morning unless you're in prison.

Lying to yourself is the perfect solution to all of your problems.

People that don't like crowds are my kind of people. Too bad all of us getting together is totally out of the question.

Before your next physical, memorize the symptoms of a serious disease, and relay them to your doctor as if you are experiencing them. When your physician suggests tests and medications, go along with it. You can always cancel the tests, and sell the pills…unless of course, the pills are keepers.

Having sex with a married person is acceptable, as long as you understand that their spouse will probably not allow them to stay overnight.

Peer pressure is not as painful as hemorrhoids.

If you're looking for an easy way to complete a work-out, feel free to substitute "Abdominal Day" with "Taking A Strenuous Shit Day."

When you go on a job interview, make sure that you are high on drugs, drunk, or both. This way, if you get the job, you're covered on all bases. The same rule applies when going to the DMV to get your updated driver's license picture.

Doing what you want to do will always take a back seat to doing what you need to do. This is important to remember while you work your mindless, going-nowhere job.

Whenever you're in doubt, ask yourself, "What would Jesus do?" (Minus, of course, that whole dying on the cross thing.)

Every once in a while, tell someone you love that they're full of shit. It'll keep them on their toes.

The pornography industry grossed over 65 billion dollars last year. Keep that in mind when your kids are choosing a career path.

If someone says, "Have a nice day," tell them to go fuck themselves. (The look on their face will be priceless.)

It's not wrong to live in the past, just as long as you die in the future.

Life's problems cannot be solved by using alcohol or drugs, but if you choose to use alcohol AND drugs, you may find a few solutions to those problems along the way.

No one ever succeeded by quitting, but they did save a lot of time.

Never cry over spilled milk. Cry over the slap you deserve, especially if you're out at an expensive restaurant ordering milk and spilling it.

If you look at the 10 Commandments as just suggestions, maybe religion isn't your thing.

If you are employed as a full-time clown....forget it. Not going to say anything about this because clowns are scarier than shit.

Don't make the same mistake twice, but if you do, make sure it is epically worse than the first one.

Use the tools that God gave you; just make sure that one of them is a shovel.

Never contribute to a cause that doesn't benefit you in some way.

If you live by the sword, you will die by the sword. (This only comes into play if you are employed as a knight at Medieval Times.)

Supporting local small businesses is a wonderful idea. It will help with the awkwardness down the line when the owner asks you to recommend a good bankruptcy attorney.

If you ever meet anyone that tells you they were abducted by aliens, ask them if they were anally probed. If they say they were not, tell them you don't believe them. If they say that they were, laugh uncontrollably and walk away.

If you are single, date the hottest person you can. If you are married, date the hottest person you can.

Trust can be earned, as long as the price is right.

Carl Friedrich Gauss (1777-1855) is considered by many to be the best mathematician of all time, but, the most significant mathematical equation in history wasn't unveiled until 1974. It was released worldwide by Billy Preston, (1946-2006) when he performed the song, *"Nothing From Nothing Leaves Nothing."*

Start a rumor about someone you dislike. If they confront you, look them straight in the eye and lie about it. Fuck them.

If you are fighting with your spouse or roommate, overeat before you go to sleep and then get into bed naked. If you die during the night, the chances of you shitting and pissing yourself are pretty good. #theyareoncleanup.

You know that you attended a tough Catholic school if a required language class was Swearing 101, and recess was spent practicing hand-to-hand combat with Sister Mary Catherine.

There's nothing wrong with acting like a fool, especially if you're an asshole.

The perfect advertising campaign for a Medical Building that leases offices to struggling Optometrists and Dentists is: "An Eye For An Eye, A Tooth For A Tooth."

The Greeks are the only ones that should be allowed to say, "It's all Greek to me."

If you arrive late and leave early, it will raise suspicion that you are experiencing explosive diarrhea.

If you emulate a movie star, an athlete, a singer or a politician, you have set your goals way too high. Start with a rich neighbor and go from there.

If your partner suggests trying something different, like you being the recipient of anal sex, explain to them that you'd rather not. (If you happen to be curious about having your rectal area invaded, please disregard this.)

If someone plays a harmless joke on you, go along with it. Then, down the line, let the air out of their car tires. When they complain, remind them that this too is also a harmless joke.

Never ask someone you don't know that well for a referral. There's usually some kind of commission in it for them.

Never leave anything better than you found it. It will be expected of you from that point on.

You reap what you sow is an old and outdated proverb. If you use it, you'll get what you deserve.

People who swear have a higher I.Q. than those who don't. #geniuslevel.

Behind every great man, there is a great woman….or two, or three.

Being the best you can be is highly overrated and takes more effort than it's worth.

Never agree to disagree with someone. It gives them the upper hand.

If you regret saying something when you're drunk, you are a coward.

Getting together with friends for dinner and drinks always sounds like a great idea, until you show up.

It's better to be safe than sorry. It is not better to be poor, stupid, and ugly than it is to be rich, smart, and beautiful. This is especially important to remember if you have absolutely no common sense.

If you decide to give money to a homeless person that carries a sign, always remember to reward their creativity accordingly.

Begin some of your future conversations by saying, "There's no easy way to tell you this."

Falling is inherently funny.

You're never really alone if you have a multiple personality disorder.

If you are feeling down in the dumps about your life, your job, your finances or your appearance, go shopping at Wal-Mart. You'll leave there feeling like a retired runway model who just won the lottery.

If you attend a wedding reception without a date, it's acceptable to leave with a member of the bridal party solely to have sex.

Always trust a gay person when it comes to opening a bottle of wine.

The power of positive thinking will get you only as far as your delusions will take you.

There are no happy endings, there are only endings. If they were happy, they would not end.

Having a hat to shit in is better than not having a pot to piss in.

The chicken did not cross the road to get to the other side. He crossed the road to get away from that finger-licking asshole, Colonel Sanders. The word from the roosters was that the Colonel enjoyed eating all species of birds, especially cocks.

The origination of the proverb, "The Best Things In Life Are Free," points to a song of the same name from the 1927 musical entitled: *"Good News."* The theme behind that song was to remind people that money and objects are not the most important things in life. Was everyone that naïve back then or were they just plain fucking stupid?

Smoking cigarettes is unhealthy. That's why there is a warning label on every pack. Taking illegal narcotics is also unhealthy, but there are no warning labels. The right thing to do would be for the drug supplier to make the drug buyer aware of this before completing the transaction. #bearesponsiblepusher.

There is a huge difference between hearing and listening. Everyone agrees with this, except deaf people.

Coming up with good ideas is like taking a healthy shit, sometimes they come to you easily, and sometimes you have to strain.

You know that you're living large if you have a kitchen drawer full of carry-out menus.

The definition of the Death Penalty is: "The punishment of execution administered to someone legally convicted of a capital crime." The definition of Marriage is: "The legally or formally recognized union of two people as partners in a personal relationship." Married people sometimes confuse these definitions because of the interchangeable words.

Instead of referring to women of a certain age as "cougars," they should be referred to as "leopards." The reasoning behind this is that leopards have colored spots on their fur, and older women have liver spots on their skin.

Opinions are like assholes, everyone has them. Assholes are like opinions, they both involve shit.

Anyone who holds a grudge against you because of something that they did to you in the first place, is an extremely confused Cocksucker.

If you believe that your best is yet to come, you are delusional. The truth of the matter is that those opportunities you once had, the dreams of wealth, and the early personal goals that you set for yourself, have all disappeared like a fart in the wind. It's time to be realistic. Move forward; preferably without the assistance of a cane or walker.

For some people, being divorced is like having the winning lottery ticket. For others, it's also like having the winning lottery ticket, but not being able to cash it in.

When you tell someone that you're going to throw-up it ruins the surprise.

If your date thinks that a manifesto is an appetizer it's a for sure sign that you're getting sex later.

If you are out in public and need to excuse yourself to go to the bathroom, impress your peers by the use of these phrases: "I have to go drain the monster." "I gotta piss like a racehorse." "I have to take a major leak." "I have to take a toxic dump." I gotta go burn a mule." "I'm gonna go drop the Cosby kids off at the pool."

There's a way to say things, and then there's a way to say things. Always choose the second one.

If you're happy and you know it and you really want to show it, if you're happy and you know it, don't clap your hands; instead drop your pants or lift your skirt. Now that's being happy.

Life is about good, bad, right, and wrong choices. What do you do when a good choice is wrong and a bad choice is right? You should make the right choice, but do it for the wrong reason. All of your bases are covered.

Many men are in search of a woman who is a cook in the kitchen, a maid in the living room, and a whore in the bedroom. Ladies, if you are all of those things; that's great, now all you have to do is to be a mechanic in the garage. #callme.

There is a fine line between what is true and what is false…it's called cocaine.

If you listen to a song or watch a movie that makes you cry, there's nothing wrong with that. It's just a reminder of what a sensitive little twat you are.

At one time or another, every guy on Earth has tried to give himself a blow job.

It doesn't matter if you've had body parts surgically added, removed, or altered, what clothes you wear, or what you've changed your name to, just please save the rest of us the time and embarrassment it takes of trying to guess which sex you are.

There's not a day that goes by, that a day doesn't go by.
#noarguementthere.

Looking up the answers to questions on Google Search makes everyone an Einstein. That poor prick had to figure everything out for himself, and then write it out longhand on a chalkboard. No wonder his hair was always so fucked up.

Most people that vote in an election will rarely admit that they chose the candidate who wound up losing.

Seeing old friends is fun, especially if they're still alive.

If someone says, "They don't make things like they used to," hit them in their forehead with your cell phone. As they regain consciousness, explain that you were just helping to prove their theory, by reminding them how much more it would've hurt if you had hit them with a rotary phone.

How come it's impossible to find names, addresses, and phone numbers for secret societies?

Everyone is Irish on St. Patrick's Day, except the Italians. They're still Italian.

Most married couples admit that the best sex that they ever had was not with their current spouse, although no one is quite sure who they're admitting that to.

There is no reason to fear death; its life that should scare the living shit out of you.

How come members of the Ku Klux Klan have never been accused of racial profiling?

Any place that is only a stone's throw away is just too fucking close unless it's a whore house, a bar, or a casino.

Heart attacks and cancer are the two leading causes of death in the United States. Suicide, diabetes, stroke, kidney failure, and Alzheimer's disease are also in the Top 10. It looks like alcohol poisoning and fatal vehicle crashes are going to have to step up their games.

Anyone who says that they think the world of you, needs to be a little more specific; are they talking Ethiopia or Hawaii?

Do people that have had their legs amputated ever use the phrase, "If the shoe fits, wear it?"

Those who know right from wrong are the most boring people in the world.

Never laugh at crippled people; unless they slip and fall. (That's some forever funny shit.)

If your last name is Dick, and you name your daughter and son Mylene and Harry, you should not only be arrested, but you should have a fund set aside for the years of therapy that they will need, especially when they're introduced as Mylene and Harry Dick.

It's always a shame to hear about the death of someone you know, especially if they owed you money.

Fool me once, shame on you. Fool me twice, shame on me. Fool me three times, and I guess it's pretty obvious who the asshole is.

Why bother to pay attention to anything that is the least of your problems?

Don't let friends drive (your car) drunk.

If you are telling a story, and use the phrase, "God Forbid" in any part of it, you're a good Catholic and excused from attending Mass for the next four Sundays. #Godsaysso.

Raise your children by loving, caring, helping, and listening to them. Later in life, when you need them the most, this could be mean the difference between your enrollment in a clean nursing facility, or being tossed into a homeless shelter with your pants full of shit.

Be the friend that your friends have to warn their friends about.

Being needy and being greedy is sometimes the same thing.

Being unlucky in love is not worse than being unlucky at Russian roulette.

If you are rummaging through loose change, maxing out your credit cards, or dipping into your rapidly depleted savings account to pay your monthly bills, the rest of us welcome you to the Shit-Show Club.

The stereotyping of people based on their ethnicity, sexual orientation, or religious beliefs, is still the funniest type of humor on the planet.

Instead of having diplomas hanging on the walls of their offices, doctors should display their medical school class rank, and the number of patients they have misdiagnosed.

Handjobs transcend all cultural barriers. Let's band together to make them the universal handshake.

Only your true-blue friends will offer you a "reach around" during a dating dry spell.

Your eyes may get weaker as you get older, but they get stronger when it comes to seeing through people's bullshit.

If you steal pennies, you will die penniless; and forever be remembered as the cheapest, stupidest fucking thief in history.

If you're in Paris having a conversation with a French person, and they inadvertently swear, do they say, "Pardon my English?"

When a one-armed man robs a bank without carrying a weapon, is it still referred to as an unarmed robbery?

How come you always see photographs of rich, fat, unattractive men with beautiful women, but you never see rich, fat, unattractive women with handsome men?

If you have an epiphany during sex, and your partner has an epiphany while eating, you should both consider having your meals in the bedroom. #specialsauceforeveryone.

When a fat person is struggling with dieting, the word "portion" is just as offensive to them, as the word "cunt" is to your girlfriend, when you introduce her to your parents.

If you're still posting your displeasure on social media about the series ending episodes of *The Sopranos* and *Game of Thrones*, it's time for you to get the fuck over it. #nomorecableforyou.

If someone says you rub them the wrong way, reach inside of their pants and ask for instructions on doing it correctly.

With the vast legalization of marijuana in the United States, it's only a matter of time before we begin to see national advertising campaigns and televised commercials. Have fun explaining this, parents of small children.

It should be mandatory for people over the age of 50 to complete a course in basic hygiene.

Chicago has become so dangerous, that multiple branches of the military are considering sending their recruits there for basic training.

Let's face it; the only way to kill two birds with one stone is if they're fucking.

White-Americans are afraid of African-Americans, African-Americans are afraid of Hispanics, Hispanics are afraid of Chinese, Chinese are afraid of Yugoslavians, Yugoslavians are afraid of Japanese, Japanese are afraid of Russians, Russians are afraid of Irish, Irish are afraid of Albanians, Albanians are afraid of Jews, Jews are afraid of Germans, Germans are afraid of Italians, and Italians are afraid of their Mothers.

Overeating is only a problem if you run out of food.

Some male inmates find Jesus when they're in prison, others find their cell mate's penis buried inside of their ass.

You'll never be considered a racist, as long as you hate all races equally.

If you want to see just how out of touch you are with current music, watch the *VH1*, *MTV*, or *Grammy Music Awards*. Unless there is an older recipient of a Lifetime Achievement Award, the chances of you knowing any singers or musical groups presenting or receiving awards are next to nothing. It's not the worst thing in the world, considering that most of the music made since 1985 is total shit anyway.

Many men would not mind being referred to as "pussy-whipped," as long as it involved them being whipped by actual pussies.

It's a medical fact that cracking your knuckles makes them bigger. Women should not refer to this as a method for breast enhancement, and men should not refer to this as a method for penis enlargement.

Is it blasphemy, or is it a compliment if someone asks you about your relationship with Jesus Christ, and you respond by calling them a "Jesus Freak?"

If you are selling something to a male dwarf, and he offers you less than your asking price, is it acceptable to accuse him of low-balling?

Overreacting to an allergic reaction does not make you a reactionary.

If you are involved in something, and the chances of success are slim and none, choose none. This will make it appear as if you knew what you were doing in the first place.

If you identify with any of the characters on the TV show *Friends*, we cannot be friends.

Having delusions of grandeur is better than having optical illusions.

Next time you board a plane, think about this: You're about to be speeding down the runway at 180 miles per hour while sitting inside a metal tube weighing 175,000 pounds (including fuel) and you're climbing to roughly 35,000 feet in the air. Have a safe flight.

If you have young children, teach them how to swear using the correct verbiage. If trouble at their school arises because of this, you can point out to their teacher or principal that you're a stickler for proper English.

If eating healthier for you involves adding things to your diet, go for it. If it involves removing foods that you enjoy eating from your diet, disregard it. Take one step at a time.

You can only be responsible for things that are within your control. So, the next time someone tells you that you are out of control, answer them by saying you are not responsible.

Making a list of things to do is the same thing as not doing them.

It is rude, ignorant, and hurtful when someone refers to the ugly stereotyping regarding the frugalness of Jewish people, by insinuating that they have big noses because the air is free. If you know anything about their wonderful heritage, you would know that they have big noses because they can fit more nickels in there.

It's a win/win if you go to a whore house on Halloween and yell, "Trick or treat!"

The medical profession needs to upgrade its creative process when it comes to assigning names to new illnesses and diseases. Nothing beats those great old-school terms like leprosy, tuberculosis, mumps, dropsy, diphtheria, croup, decrepitude, grocer's itch, lumbago, trench mouth, and an all-time favorite, scurvy.

When a man blows his nose, does his penis get jealous?

If someone refers to you as a diamond in the rough, they are insinuating that you currently resemble a lump of coal. This is not a compliment.

Are over-sensitive African-Americans doubly offended if you tell them an off-color joke?

If you are sick, you're only confusing your body by feeding a cold and starving a fever.

Dropping LSD in the comfort of your own home while watching the original versions of these movies will alter your life: *The Wizard Of Oz, Willy Wonka & The Chocolate Factory, The Grand Budapest Hotel, Blade Runner, The Shining, Fear And Loathing In Las Vegas (1998), Jacob's Ladder, The Matrix, Alien, Beetlejuice, Brazil, Pink Floyd's The Wall, Inception, The Time Machine, Fantasia, 2001 A Space Odyssey, Apocalypse Now, Dune,* **and** *Time Bandits.* **Enjoy your trip!**

If you are not satisfied with a customer service representative because they referred to you as "Chief," is it acceptable to shoot them with a bow and arrow?

Being in the wrong place at the right time is much more fun than being in the right place at the wrong time.

House flies are the Jehovah's Witnesses of bugs.

One of the biggest problems that bald males have is not knowing when to stop washing their faces.

You can rest assured that a fat chef has honed their craft.

You know that you've reached adulthood, when breakfast consists of having your cake and eating it too.... in the bedroom, naked, while smoking weed, while watching the 60-inch HDTV that you bought hot, with your illegal cable hook up, while drinking orange juice and vodka, and so on, and so on, and so on.

If you refer to smoking a cigarette as ingesting the darkness of a smoky teat, it's time to consider quitting.

If you are asked a question, and the answer is "yes," just simply answer "yes." Don't answer the question with one of those rhetorical questions that imply "yes," like: "Is the Pope Catholic?" "Does a bear shit in the woods?" "Does Rose Kennedy own a black dress?"

I could care less if the correct way to express caring less is by saying, "I couldn't care less."

If you walk backward and take one step forward and two steps backward, you'll be confused; but you may also get to your destination quicker, depending on which way you're headed. #I'mfuckingdizzy.

Do not refer to your chronic masturbation as a "Job Skill" when filling out an application for employment.

Clemenza, from the movie, *The Godfather* was wrong. You should leave the cannolis, and take the gun. You could always go back later to rob the bakery shop.

Being unemployed is better than being unemployable.

You haven't lived life to the fullest until you've suffered a nervous breakdown.

Imagine the pandemonium and outrage in the next 10 years, when it's revealed that the use of our microwave ovens causes cancer. #waitandsee.

Whisper more, people equate that shit with being mysterious.

Monogamy is too cruel of a rule.

You should consider getting out and about more if your weekend revolves around the excitement of home-delivered Chinese food.

If you take pride in the way you easily relate to people, try having a garage sale. By the end of the day, you will acquire a true hatred for every multi-colored cheapskate that sets foot upon your driveway.

You know that you're in a comfortable sexual relationship with your partner if you refer to each other's genitalia with nicknames.

Ask someone out on a date that doesn't speak your language. If your attempt at doing this is successful, and they show up, ask them for sex. (Hey, when you're on a roll, you're on a roll.)

Bowling is the gutter ball of all sports.

Writing a blog is about as pretentious as a person could get. #nobodygivestwofuckingshitswhatyou think.

Being anal-retentive about your desk at work is better than being anal-retentive about the toilet seat at work.

Guys should offer to mow their single female neighbor's lawn just to see if she's into hidden meanings.

Viewing pornography on the internet is a superhighway rite of passage.

Before blowing out the candles on their birthday cake, do people with suicidal tendencies make a death wish first?

Even if someone is stupid, they should know the difference between mine and yours.

If you send someone you don't know all that well a Facebook friend request, don't expect them to accept it if you use your police mug shot as your profile picture.

Men with only one testicle should refrain from saying, "Have a ball."

Ill-fitting toupees are at their funniest when exposed to inclement weather.

Dentists are to men, what gynecologists are to women, but the chairs are different.

Are hungry, goofy gay men who eat Fruit Loops cereal for breakfast just starving for attention?

If somebody has done you wrong in your life, you should be the bigger person, and consider burying the hatchet...RIGHT IN THE MIDDLE OF THEIR FUCKING FOREHEAD!

Before advertising new medications on television, the laboratories should focus more on the plethora of side effects that they have, especially when the spokesperson points out that after taking the medicine, there are possibilities of contracting kidney failure, blindness, bloody anal secretion, heart attack, loss of hearing, liver damage, and cancer.

Three Dog Night was wrong. One is not the loneliest number, zero is. Always has been, always will be.

What scared the shit out of chickens so much that their breed of bird is universally known as the standard way to describe being afraid?

When someone orders a steak cooked well-done it should negatively affect their credit score.

If your boss offers you a pay increase, and you refuse it to show your commitment as a true advocate of the company, you can always look forward to winning "The Asshole of the Year" award at the Christmas party.

Impressionists that don't impress have been known to leave a bad impression.

Auto alarms can be bypassed by most car thieves. Just apply a sticker that says you have an alarm, it'll drive them nuts when they try to look for it.

When a tough guy tells you that you have only two options, look him straight in the eye and tell him that you want the third one.

Count Dracula, The Wolf Man, and Frankenstein all had real names. How come The Mummy and The Creature From The Black Lagoon got fucked-over in that department?

Sometime, very shortly, instead of getting flowers as a gift, female weed enthusiasts will be receiving bouquets of marijuana. (You heard it here first.)

It's been said that right before you die, you will receive total consciousness and your whole life will flash right before your very eyes. That God, what a jokester!

No rest for the wicked means there are a lot of wide-awake mother fuckers out there.

The two types of vehicle collisions gay males don't mind are, "head-on" and "rear end."

If something is easier said than done, say it to as many people as you can. Then, when some other asshole does it, you take the credit for it.

If your regular doctor sends your rectal x-rays to a proctologist that you've never met, and then when you do meet him, the very first thing out of his mouth after he performs your anal examination is to say that your x-rays don't do you justice…I'd worry about that.

The inevitability of the inevitable is inevitably inevitable. (Whatever the fuck that means.)

Since it seems that every job on the planet doesn't require you be a rocket scientist, exactly what job is it that being a rocket scientist is a necessary prerequisite for employment consideration?

Some sex phrases that involve animal noises are: barking like a dog, squealing like a pig, howling like a wolf, cooing like a bird, roaring like a tiger, and purring like a kitten. (Somewhere out there, I'm pretty confident that some pig moos like a cow.) #didyouseewhatIdidthere? #twoanimalnoisesforthepriceofone.

If someone you haven't seen for a while says, "You're still as beautiful (or as handsome) as ever," what they mean is that you've aged. (You need to see through that type of bullshit immediately, if not sooner.)

When the waiter at an expensive restaurant describes a menu item as the pièce de résistance, don't be a rube, order it. This is your chance to show off your worldly knowledge of fine cuisine. When it arrives at your table, nod in approval, applaud and then ask for ketchup.

When you're told something is 100% for sure, believe it. If you're told it is 1000% for sure, it's a lie.

Who wears popped-up collars? Count Dracula, Elvis Presley, and Assholes do. Which one are you?

When blind people attend sporting events or concerts, how do they know if they have bad seats?

The food at The Olive Garden is to the Italians, what toilet paper is to an ass crack.

Before you sell your soul to the devil, make sure to check eBay first to see what they're going for.

There's nothing wrong with mixing apples and oranges, just don't mix cherries and broccoli. That's some nasty shit right there.

Swearing has its benefits, especially when you're at a loss for words.

If you can do anything I can do better, by all means, have at it. (If you need me, I'll be masturbating on the couch, eating pizza, and watching Netflix.)

People who are always smiling have something to hide. No one is that fucking happy on purpose.

Think before you speak. (Not one person does this.)

Going on a date when you're over the age of 50, is like having appointments with your dentist and proctologist both on the same day. It's all about how you open up.

Is the fear of phobias called phobia phobia?

Peeple that misuze and misspell werds, our topically more dummer than knot.

If someone's ass is grass, why the fuck would you want to be the lawnmower? #youareanasstrimmer.

Saving money for your retirement is about as realistic as spending money is when you retire.

Fat people who bet their asses have much more to lose.

Escape Rooms are the new 60-90 minute live-action/team-based game where people meet at a facility that offers theme-designed rooms to solve puzzles, discover clues, and perform tasks to accomplish the specific goal of escaping in a limited amount of time. Little does everyone know that we've all been playing the Escape Room game for years, we know it as Holiday Dinner in the Dining Room with Our Family.

Life has a funny way of lining up bear traps when you put your best foot forward.

It's not a problem if you rob Peter to pay Paul unless you're Peter. And if you are Peter, you can always borrow from Paul because he'll be sympathetic when he hears that some asshole just robbed you.

Too much of a good thing is a bad thing, but only if the good thing winds up being a bad thing because it was too much of a good thing to start with. Good thing we straightened that out before it became a bad thing.

If Hasbro and Fisher-Price had made sex toys for baby boomers when they were growing up, there would be no such thing today as an LGBTQ movement.

Why is it when women in movies get kissed, they don't bend their leg at the knee anymore like they used to do in those older movies?

Is Witchcraft an acceptable hobby for young girls that aren't into sports or music?

Meteorologists that are in the winter of their lives, but still have a spring in their step after they fall, is primarily due to all of those years of being wrongly accused of having clouded judgment when all they had were sunny dispositions.

If you've ever been out driving and pulled your vehicle alongside a bunch of Hispanics listening to their car radio, you are probably fully aware that there is no such thing as sad Mexican music.

Why is it that only the bad shit in life goes around and comes around?

When someone gives up smoking cigarettes, you should congratulate them on their healthy accomplishment, but not before you mutter, "quitter" under your breath.

If you share something in confidence with someone about a bad or inappropriate thing that you've done, and they tell you that it's not the worst thing in the world that they've ever heard, should you feel good because it wasn't that bad, or should you feel bad because you could've done a better job at it being worse?

Don't feel sad when you see movie stars and entertainers that you haven't seen for a while, and they've noticeably aged poorly. If they knew you, they'd probably feel the same way.

If you look the other way when someone is up to no good, you'll never learn.

Whatever happened to the world's need for ditch diggers?

If the majority of your income is based on the ratings you receive from customers, you need to quit and find something else to do. All customers are Jagoffs.

Why do people wish to have a dog's life if a dog works like a dog, gets sick as a dog, and then dies like a dog?

Since no one seems to have one, where exactly in the human body is the jealousy bone located?

The worst thing about cooking is having to cook.

If bullshit were flowers, there'd be a shitload of florists.

Wishing someone good luck when you secretly hope that they fail, is only a contradiction if you can't keep a secret.

Can crabs catch a case of the crabs?

Engaged couples that expect their wedding guests to incur a huge travel and lodging expense to some out of state or exotic out of the country location just to watch them get married are selfish, delusional, and truly do deserve each other. #theywillbedivorcedinayear.

Ali MacGraw, the actress from the 1970 movie, *Love Story*, delivered to all theatergoers one of the most memorable movie lines ever, when she told costar Ryan O'Neil, "Love means never having to say you're sorry." Is there any doubt that if that movie was made today, that line would be changed to, "Love means always having to say you're sorry?"

If the number 666 is the sign of the beast, is the number 69 the sign of things to come?

Not quite sure why the Grim Reaper is always so grim. He doesn't have to buy clothes because he always wears the same black cloak, he carries a nice sharp scythe and a cool hourglass, he collects souls (which can't weigh that much), and business is always good.

If you think that you know the inner you, the next time you're alone, instead of reading something to yourself; try reading it out loud.

You can tell all that you need to know about a person, by whether they bring the banana to their mouth or their mouth to the banana.

Tattoos and beards don't make you tough unless you're a woman.

Consider writing to Congress, and demand that a form of "street justice punishment" be put into law for all of those found guilty of a heinous crime against children, women, and the elderly. The punishment should be administered to the guilty by members of the affected families. If the victims choose not to take part in this type of retribution, a public lottery should be offered for those that wish to carry this out themselves. It should be broadcast live on pay-per-view, with a portion of the proceeds given to the victim, or their families. After all, there's only so much that you can watch on Netflix.

The little things in life only count if they add up to big things.

Polish people have been the target of cheap jokes for years. Unfortunately, it didn't help matters much, when the police recently found the skeletal remains of Godzislaw Porchonski kneeling in the corner of a dark closet in a vacant building. After a thorough investigation, authorities discovered that the last time anyone saw Mr. Porchonski alive, was when he began his competition in the 1998 Hide-N-Go-Seek Championship. The good news is that he was posthumously awarded the first place trophy. Congratulations and Rest In Peace, Godzislaw!

If dreams did come true, there would be an overpopulation problem in hell, jail, and the insane asylum.

If someone makes you a job offer that sounds too good to be true, it probably is. If it was that good, they would've taken it for themselves, or offered it to an in-law of the boss.

If you're trying to get over the break-up of your previous relationship, have rebound sex with a relative or friend of your former partner. You'll feel better in no time.

Overweight people that use mobile shopping carts just because they're fat should be restricted from going down the snack food aisles.

If you write something worth reading about or do something worth writing about, you will suffer the consequences.

Gluten has been in all different types of foods for years, and peanuts have been around since Adam and Eve fed them to the dinosaurs. Why is it that all of a sudden, every other kid on the planet can't have a handful of fucking peanuts without going into a coma? Also, why are grown-ass adults that look like they are on death's door, crying like a gaggle of little bitches when they can't get a gluten-free meal?

Besides bearing a striking resemblance to one of your aunts, the bearded lady at the circus was more of a distraction than an attraction.

Can you think of anyone that you like better when they're drunk?

On top of serving a jail sentence, wealthy people that have been convicted of cheating the IRS should be assigned a minimum wage job to pay back taxes and fines. #fuckthoserichassholes.

Cuddling with your partner is overrated unless it leads to an oral episode.

You will not be successful at losing weight if you add ice cream and chocolate syrup to your Slim Fast.

You can choose your friends, but you can't choose your family. If you are too stupid to realize this very obvious statement, you don't deserve to have either of them.

"The Luck of the Irish" phrase dates back to the second half of the 19th Century when some of the world's most successful gold and silver miners were of Irish or Irish American descent. The luck thing must be true. After all, how many Irish people do you know that are currently working in mines for a living?

There is no "I" in team, but there is a "U" in cunt.

If you're Catholic, just for fun on the next religious holiday, go to a local 7-11 with a cashier that is noticeably from India. Buy something, pay for it, and as you're leaving; wish them a Merry Christmas or a Happy Easter. It drives them fucking crazy.

If the highest political office in your country is held by a man or woman whose title is King, Queen, Prince, Princess, Duke, Duchess, Emperor, Empress, or Prime Minister, it's time to move.

If you can recall who your first kiss was with, how it was, and where you were when it happened, you are a true romantic at heart. (Just don't share that information with anyone because it's creepy that you still remember.)

If the game plan of your life is to draw your last breath as you spend your last buck, you will probably be remembered as a rebel's rebel; and not too fucking bright.

Did any of those ego-inflated, self-important actors, actresses, and entertainers that promised to move out of the country if Donald Trump became President move out? If they didn't, that's okay; they'll have another opportunity to do so when he wins again in 2020, and maybe this time they can take Trump with them, and truly make America great again. #assholefreezone.

When dining out, always overtip your server, even if the service wasn't great. You have no idea the type of high-quality assholes that waiters and waitresses have to serve food and drinks daily.

The next time you kill a bee, remember that they are the only species of insects that produce food for humans. You should also remember that flies spread diseases and eat shit. #swatwiselyplease.

You haven't experienced true heartbreak, until you've been thinking about leftovers all day, only to come home and find out that someone has already eaten them.

Facebook's basic reaction emojis look exactly like a relationship from start to finish.

Does the verse, "Love Thy Neighbor as Thyself" mean you should share a mutual masturbatory session with them, or does it mean more like inviting them over for a barbeque? Either way, I'll bring the sausage.

Those that jog instead of run have been known to apply that lazy method of exercising to all other aspects of their lives.

The file cabinet in Hell is filled with the good intentions of its inhabitants.

If Canada was a beer, it would be called America Lite.

If you blame yourself when something doesn't go right, you are automatically guilty by association.

When Godspeed is wished, do The Flash & Superman get jealous?

The proof is in the pudding, right next to Bill Cosby's dick.

The Top Ten biggest bull-shitters by their profession:

1. Politicians.

2. Religious Clergy.

3. Car Salespeople.

4. Psychiatrists & Psychologists.

5. Lawyers.

6. Journalists/News Media.

7. Insurance Salespeople.

8. Prostitutes.

9. Store/Shop Owners.

10. Stockbrokers.

Unhappy couples that need to save money on airline tickets should consider temporarily putting their differences aside; toss a coin, and the loser register for the flight as a service animal.

There is nothing feminine or sanitary about a woman's period napkin.

Long nose hairs are always funny.

Your Facebook friends are secretly making fun of you when you post pictures of your cat.

Invisible people are unable to hide in plain sight.

A few handfuls of something are absolutely nothing compared to a shitload.

If God is all-forgiving, suffering the wrath of God shouldn't be too awful bad. Carry on with your debauchery.

If judging a book by its cover means the same to you as judging a person by their clothes, you are a shallow-minded nitwit.

People that live in filthy homes rarely have to worry about unexpected company.

There is nothing sexier than a woman who calls her man, "baby," unless she's referring the size of his genitalia.

If you're up for a good challenge, be prepared for a bitter defeat, said every pessimist ever. #losermentality.

Who are the assholes that ruin a good cake by walking through it?

Ages 65 and up are referred to as "The Golden Years." What the fuck is so golden about being that old?

Some people are destined to never reach their full potential in life. If you are one of those people, it means that you are a failure. Congratulations, you have found your destiny.

Having consensual sex with someone that you don't know is a great way to meet new people.

If there is blood in your urine or stool, there's no need to panic; it just means that you're dying. We all die.

All drugs are dangerous except the ones that make you feel really good. If at all possible, buy those fuckers by the pound because real life sucks.

How does a man going to bed early and getting up early, make him healthy, wealthy and wise? If anything, it makes him sickly, poor and stupid.

If someone asks what you bring to the table, your reply should be, "My appetite."

If you cannot be good, you might as well be bad. This is the best advice you could ever give or receive.

On December 25th, Christians celebrate the birth of Jesus. On what day do Satanists celebrate the birth of Lucifer? #happybirthdaySatan.

Explaining the facts of life to your children is part of responsible parenting. Explaining to them why some men dress as women, or why some women dress as men, is describing Halloween to them.

If you are not currently in a relationship with anyone, you should practice breaking up with yourself.

Shaking hands is an acceptable way to share an informal greeting between two people. Bowing and curtsying are acceptable ways to share formal greetings. A new and widely popular greeting that is rapidly becoming both informally and formally acceptable is to do these three things ALL at once to another person: A wet-willy, a noogy, and a titty twister. (Be honest, you just thought about yourself greeting someone this way, and it became a hell of a lot funnier.)

Heavy is the ass that wears a fanny pack.

Prostitution is a misunderstood profession.

If highly toxic biological waste is found in your stool, ripping ass may be cause for Nuclear Proliferation.

The use of the "thumbs up" and "thumbs down" emojis have saved countless hours of unnecessary texting and verbal communication between human beings.

"Know Your Enemy as You Know Yourself." Boy, that Sun Tzu must have been a fucking riot to hang out with.

All young children are addicted to empty cardboard boxes.

If you think going back in time will change who you are or what you have become, you're wrong. Those things will not change. What will also not change is the fact that you're an asshole for thinking you can go back in time.

Coincidence and fate are often confused, just like stupidity and ignorance. Here's an example: "It's not a coincidence that you're stupid and ignorant, it's fate."

Being able to change the pitch, length, and sound of your fart or burp makes you an automatic candidate for the "Life of the Party" award.

You know that you have a lot of secrets if there's a need to color coordinate the skeletons in your closet.

Anyone who uses their fingers in midair to physically describe quotation marks, to emphasize a word, or a phrase during a face to face verbal conversation, deserves to have their eyes poked out with said fingers.

Your overuse of duct tape is God's way of telling you that you're a shitty repair person.

When someone says, "we'll see," it means, "no."

Co-workers that consistently share meals are plotting something. Management needs to search their desks and lockers.

They call it "falling" in love because when you fall, you get hurt.

If you're divorced, it should be mandatory that the theme song from the movie, "*The Exorcist*," be used as the cell phone ring tone for your former spouse.

There should be a Bogeywoman. (Equal rights and all.)

When someone says, "They died before their time," it's because the deceased was young. That does not mean it's acceptable to say, "It's about time," when someone you don't like finally dies.

When you furrow your untrimmed unibrow, it resembles the Gaza Strip.

Do male Smurfs know when they have blue balls?

Excluding Charles Manson and his group, hippies weren't all that bad.

Asking a prospective employer for a management position in the Anger Department will not get you hired.

The main difference between being a prisoner and being a professor is one person has numbers after their name, and the other one has letters.

If 90% of your social media posts are pictures of you posing with an alcoholic beverage at home, at a bar, on vacation, in your back yard, in a pool, at a restaurant, at a sporting event, on a boat, at a concert, at a wedding, or at a party, you most definitely have a drinking problem, and I also want to hang out with you.

Fat, shirtless bald guys that wear gold chains and smoke cigars, all look alike.

If you're having a tough time controlling your anger at work, try replacing "fuck you" with "ok great."

A coma is God's way of providing you with much-needed rest.

Who owns lucky stars, and then thanks them?

As time goes on, your memory becomes confabulated. In your mind, the older you get, the better you were. There's no need to worry. The rest of us will always remember that you weren't that great, to begin with.

If you can sleep through the night without the aid of a pill, and don't wake up until the alarm clock goes off in the morning, you have a severe health crisis and need to see your physician as soon as possible. #youarenotfuckinghuman. #atleastgetuptopeeforchristsakes.

Whoever has the lap that is luxury, please allow us all to have a seat. (We'll grind and dry-hump you if that makes your decision easier.)

Facebook posts that ask you to type "Amen" in the comment section are messages that originated from Satan. It makes it easier for him to find you.

Guys, if you find a woman who eats chicken wings like she's trying to kill the bird again, marry her.

If you're not happy with yourself, look in the mirror. That's your reflection you see. That's who you should blame, and that's who you should point your finger at. Now, I'm your fucking life coach.

Like, luck, love, lick, and lust. The letter "L" does not fuck around.

If happiness is the new rich, inner peace is the new success, health is the new wealth, and kindness is the new cool, why are most of us broke, alone, sick, and unpopular? #itisaloselosesituation.

When you tell some of the posers that pass themselves off as your friends about something good that concerns you; regardless of their fake-ass initial congratulatory reaction, more than half of them will not be happy for you. Remember this the next time you decide to share that type of news with those insanely jealous and bitter strokes.

For the record, you are not as anything as you used to be.

No matter what you do in life, always give 100%, unless you're donating blood.

To be socially sensitive to people who are fat, but identify as slender, they will now be referred to as Trans-Slender.

If you're still waiting for your moment in the spotlight, don't you worry; it's coming soon. It'll be right above you in the basement of the funeral home when you're laid out on that metal slab as the embalmer prepares you for your wake.

Being "asked" to do something versus being "told" to do something is the difference of whether or not it will be done.

If you have a secret crush on someone, keep it to yourself. Your fantasies will be forever grateful that you did.

Why was it when we were growing up and our parents told us: "There's more where that came from," it was never anything good, and it usually involved a crack, a smack, or a biff in the head?

If you dance like nobody's watching, you're wrong. Everyone is watching, and they're laughing their fucking asses off. They're laughing because you're probably white, drunk, overweight, and dance like a Parkinson's patient being stung by a swarm of bees during an earthquake.

There is no fast food sandwich that looks as good when you purchase it as it does in the television commercial.

You can talk all that you want to about core values, integrity, morals, righteousness, and trustworthiness; but in the end, money always wins.

If running out of time is a major concern of yours, the sand granules in your hourglass have already passed from top to bottom. You. Are. Over.

When asked what they do for a living, beware of those that say, "I serve at the pleasure of," and then give the name of their employer. These people are corporate assassins. They perform the dirty, illegal, and unscrupulous tasks for the company they work for. These individuals are without conscience, and you should avoid any future communication or involvement with them. In simpler terms, they are the boss's suck-holes.

If you take it personally when a character on one of your favorite television programs is killed, or written off of the show, you need to adjust your meds.

If you had a dollar every time someone said if they had a dollar for something, you'd be ass-deep in dollar bills, just like your baby sister who works at the Strip Club.

People will always talk shit about you, but when they criticize your family, your cooking, or your music, the time has come to throw them a severe beating.

If you think that the right to bear arms means it's acceptable to wear a sleeveless shirt, there's a job that has a broom and a shovel with your name on them.

If you have been called irrational, and you're not quite sure what that means, you will surely solidify that evaluation of you, if you think that applying a soothing ointment to your anus will cure it.

Does anyone know what the final verdicts were on all those federal cases that people made out of insignificant problems?

If you are clueless, is it ok to ask for a hint?

If you refer to marijuana as the toothpaste of the soul, you may have a touch of Rastafarian in your DNA.

Sometimes, saying that you're sorry is the right thing to do. Other times, not saying anything is the right thing to do. For all of those times in between, just say, "fuck it" and be done with it.

Before you make an offer to drive an overweight relative or friend somewhere, you should do the following: Check how far back you can move your passenger side seat, get a professional evaluation on your vehicle suspension, and check the air pressure in your tires. On second thought, you might be better off just meeting them there. #callU-hallfatass.

Why is it when you break up with someone, within the next month they morph into a hot date piece?

Do you know why archeologists have never unearthed human remains that they could not positively identify as a male or a female? It's because those are the only two fucking choices there are, that's why.

Parents that do not conduct themselves accordingly at their son or daughter's sporting events, should be forced to run sprints after the game while wearing their child's uniform.

If you allowed conflicting political views to ruin a friendship or a relationship, you are a bigger asshole than the political party or politicians that you were arguing about.

What the hell is wrong with "well enough," that we're always being told to leave it alone?

What do turkeys eat on Thanksgiving?

There are two kinds of pain in this world, pain that hurts, and pain that alters. They both suck.

If you are out at a club and have had way too much to drink, there is no doubt that you have at least one more bad decision in your very near future. Cheers!

I don't mind holding a door open for an older person, or waiting an extra minute or two at a stop sign as the elderly slowly walk across, but if they don't start exhibiting a little more hustle, that polite and respectful shit is gonna come to an abrupt end.

"Go Big Or Go Home," is not a good advertising slogan for Jenny Craig Weight Loss Clinic.

Was does James Bond always introduce himself by giving his last name first, and then follow it with his entire name? #fuckingsuaveass007.

If an alien race is monitoring television broadcast signals from Earth, and they happen to be watching our reality television shows, they must be laughing their pointed heads and concave gray asses off at us.

Men will never understand women. A woman could love a man to death one day, and the next day, it could be the last time she ever speaks to him.

"Putting Lipstick on a Pig" is a rhetorical expression. It is used to convey the message that making cosmetic or superficial changes, is a futile attempt to disguise the true nature of a product or person. That being said, what was that shade of lipstick your date wore last weekend? I couldn't tell because her snout covered most of it up.

The truth will not set you free if you are a liar, it will only complicate things.

Facebook does a shitty job with "Suggested Friends" and "People You May Know" sections. If they wanted to be helpful, they should offer these choices: "People You Should Avoid" and "Friends That You Used To Know, But Don't Care About Anymore."

The saying: "Seek, and Ye Shall Find," does not apply to lost car keys.

If your parents ever used the phrase, "keep talking," you knew it meant to shut the fuck up.

"Tit for tat," does not sound like it would be a good deal for any woman.

A man knows that he can trust his wife to be a good mother if she freely admits stealing batteries out of their child's toy for her vibrator.

Since its football season, here's a reminder to all of you poor spellers out there: It's "lose," not "loose."

If you're bored, type this question in Google Search: "Why were cornflakes invented?" (You're welcome, and have a good breakfast.)

Being a baby must be traumatizing. Imagine falling asleep in your warm, comfy crib surrounded by all of your favorite stuffed playthings, only to wake up with a full diaper while being pushed around in a stroller at Walmart.

My therapist once told me, "Fuck anyone that doesn't like you." (He eventually changed that suggestion after I explained to him I would need to have sex with at least 300 people.)

From now on, greet your male co-workers by asking how their cocks are doing. They will appreciate your genuine concern.

I wonder if Stevie Wonder has ever wondered why love is also blind.

Before you choose to spend the rest of your life with someone, picture whether or not they would be the type to gently wipe your ass after you accidentally crapped in your pants, or would they be the type to drag you in the backyard and hose you down like a fucking circus animal.

Remember that spelling rule "I" before "E?" I guess they forgot about that weird, foreign neighbor Keith. He received eight beige sleighs from feisty, caffeinated weightlifters.

A recent study shows that there are more germs on the average cell phone than there are on the average toilet seat. That's probably because most people talk out of their asses.

The cartoon character Popeye was not the inspiration for the famous chicken franchise; it was actor Gene Hackman's portrayal of detective Jimmy "Popeye" Doyle in the 1971 Academy Award-winning movie, *The French Connection*. I guess all kids should be happy about that. It sort of serves as a "fuck you" to cartoon Popeye for the years that parents used him as an incentive for them to eat their slimy, ratty-assed spinach. (You would've thought that it was punishment enough for Popeye to have that skinny, ugly, white-trash, meth-head lookin' bitch Olive Oyl as his girlfriend.)

We're all in trouble if we are what we eat.

Ben and Jerry's ice cream is so fucking delicious, but I can't get this thought out of my head that one of their old, gray pubic hairs made its way into the pint that I'm eating.

Collecting "past due" notices should not be considered a hobby.

If you piss me off, but you are old and take blood thinners, I won't get physical with you, but I will say a prayer that you badly cut yourself the next time you shave.

Sexually aroused older men with poor memories will continue to be disappointed when they tune in to watch a rerun episode of *Leave it to Beaver*.

Why isn't there an option available to quickly cancel the delivery of sent texts and photographs, before they are seen? There isn't a person alive that hasn't regretted sending something, and then not being able to retrieve it. (Think drunken texts, dick pics, and boobs and panty shots.) It was probably far more important for those cellular tech wizards to create applications that offered more useless emojis, holiday theme borders, and multi-colored collages so users could create and send those obnoxious pictures of their pets dressed in tuxedos and party hats while smiling with human teeth.

No picture is worth a thousand words....maybe a couple of hundred at best.

Anti-guns, pro-guns, anti-abortion, pro-abortion, anti-segregation, pro-segregation...enough is fucking enough. I wish there was a country where people could vote on whether or not they want or don't want these things. #wakeuppeoplethisisAmerica.

People who rush while they shave the underside of their genitals are true risk-takers.

It's probably just a coincidence if you're constipated and someone tells you that you're full of shit.

The only person who wants to live to be 100 is a 99-year-old.

Why does freshly sliced lunch meat smell like ass?

It's almost time to imbibe in those Sexy Winter Drinks: Pert Peppermint Schnapps Nipples, Shrunken Tequila Testicles, Frozen Baileys And Cream Balls, Cold Ass Cheeks Chardonnay, Shy Peter Pumpkin Spice Cider, Wind Chilled Titties Hot Toddy, Polar Pussy Vodka Vortex, Screwing In Your Wool Pajamas Screwdriver, Too Cold To Copulate Chivas, Dick Has Disappeared Daiquiri Ice, Holiday Hand-Job Harvey Wallbanger, Santa Claus Is Coming Too Soon Sangria, Man In The Frozen Canoe Manhattan, Heavy Accumulation In Your Pants Portifino, and Freezing His Stored Nuts Off Pink Squirrel.

Why would you want to have anyone by the short hairs?

Here's some advice for Catholic parents:

If your children aren't listening to you the way that they should, remind them about the Fourth Commandment, "Honor Thy Father and Thy Mother." If that doesn't work, explain to them since no one in the house is going to follow The Ten Commandments, you will have no other alternative than to break the Fifth Commandment, "Thou Shalt Not Kill." Then, ask them to clean their rooms, do their chores, and get their homework done, or you'll have to fucking strangle them to death…in the name of Jesus Christ, our Lord, and Savior.

If you slap a two-faced person, consider yourself a successful multitasker.

I'm not quite sure who the goofs are that make up those bullshit "National" days like: "National Talk Like A Pirate Day," "National Pizza Day," and "National Underwear Day," but here's an addition that they should consider for themselves: "National I'm An Asshole For Creating Stupid Fucking Shit Like This Day."

There's a time and place for everything, this isn't the time, nor the place, there's no time like the present, time stands still for no one, it's about time….enough already! Somebody better make up their fucking mind, or shit just ain't gonna get done.

Members of the Mafia have the best nicknames.

Any guy that wears a bright, multi-colored print shirt is desperately trying to hide something, and he's using that obnoxious shirt to throw everyone off the scent.

Looking at pictures of dead relatives can be depressing. What's even more depressing is the fact that sooner or later, we will all be dead relatives, and not just in older pictures.

No matter what type of celebration you attend, the food that you're served is always more important than the actual event.

Taking a couple of hits of ecstasy before you attend a wake or a funeral is never a good idea.

Before hosting a dinner party for your neighbors, obtain a couple of photographs of a famous serial killer. Then, slide them into existing frames right alongside your current family pictures. If one of the neighbors is sharp enough to recognize the killer's photograph, and they question you about it, walk up to them slowly, get close to their face, and nervously stammer while you explain he was your confused and misguided cousin. Then smile awkwardly, walk away, and offer to refill their drink. Goodtimes.
#jeffreydahmer
#richardspeck
#charlesmanson
#johnwaynegacy
#richardramierez
#tedbundy

All of my dreams are in color. I have super strength, including the ability to fly in my dreams. I am young again in my dreams. All of my sexual fantasies with every woman I have ever had the hots for are fulfilled in my dreams. Everything is perfect in every aspect of my life in my dreams. So, how the fuck can anyone expect me to wake up every morning with a positive attitude, and carry on with my bullshit days after experiencing nights like that?

It's funny how smells trigger certain thoughts. For example, smelling garlic makes you think of Italian food, smelling curry makes you think of Indian food, and smelling shit makes you think of Congress.

"Hot mess," "train wreck," "poison," and "toxic," are often used to describe failed relationships. The funny thing is that just weeks earlier, those very same relationships were supposedly blossoming. Some of the words used at that time were, "magical," "spiritual," "forever," and "heavenly." Enjoy your emotional roller coaster ride you lovebirds, more than likely; it'll be derailing shortly.

Airports around the nation are actively attempting to discourage their passengers from smoking on the premises. Unfortunately, they are receiving a lot of pressure from tobacco lobbyists. The initial plan was to install special terminals just for smokers, but the name "Terminal Cancer" was not approved by the Federal Aviation Authority.

If you're a young to middle-aged actor, it might be a good idea to start brushing up on your characterization of mobsters. These famous movie mob guys are in their 70's and 80's: Danny Aiello, Paul Sorvino, Jack Nicholson, Robert DeNiro, Al Pacino, Harvey Keitel, Joe Pesci, and James Caan. Unless there's some kind of retirement home heist caper in the works, the ticks on their gangster clocks are just about up. #fugetaboutrememberingtheirlines. #don'tfugetabouttakingtheirmeds. #theyforgotwhatfugetaboutitmeans.

Looking through your boyfriend or girlfriend's bathroom medicine cabinet the first time you stay overnight at their place, is almost as important as your comfort level is shitting there.

If you burglarize a home in the middle of the night and then sit at the kitchen table until morning, do not expect to be served breakfast.

You should not wear a tee-shirt that says, "Underwear Is Optional" to your child or grandchild's Pre-School graduation ceremony.

Next time you get on a crowded elevator, make your way to the back corner, sit on the floor, take out your phone, put it to your ear, and pretend like there is someone on the other end. Then, shout into it, "Ten-Four Mission Control, I'm ready for take-off."

Comfortable sexual positions should not be a topic of conversation at a church luncheon.

Ever since I read that eating pineapple makes a man's semen taste sweet, my kitchen has been stocked like a fucking Hawaiian luau. (Single guys should always be prepared for a chance sexual encounter.) You married guys don't have to worry about that. From what I've heard, most of you haven't been blown since two weeks after your honeymoon. By the way, you guys may also want to question your wives about the abundance of cucumbers in the house, especially since she hasn't made a salad in months.

The longer you wait; your good ideas will eventually evolve into bad ideas. Procrastination could save you from failure, embarrassment, and jail.

If a physical altercation suddenly breaks out in your living room while your guests are watching a football game, is it acceptable to punch one of your in-laws in the throat if they were in the kitchen at the time the fight broke out?

Years ago, I dated a girl who was a twin. I remember how people used to ask me how I was able to tell them apart. It was never really that difficult since Sharon's hair was blonde, and her twin Steve had a cock.

If you drink expensive bottled water, your urine might be worth a few bucks. Start saving it for a rainy day, just in case.

The next time you're at the mall, go to the perfume kiosk and ask the salesperson what fragrance they would recommend for an elderly woman. When they show you a couple of bottles or offer you a sample whiff, ask which one of the selections they would recommend to hide the smells of body odor and diarrhea. (Let's see just how badly they want that sale.)

If evolution is Satan's plan to deny the existence of God, what is God's plan to deny the existence of Satan? I'm one of the last people to suggest anything to the Almighty, but I think it's long overdue for Him to send at least a reminder of who He is…maybe something simple; like one of those turning water into wine deals. Better hurry, God; I think that prick Lucifer is ahead in the polls.

Made in the USA
Monee, IL
10 December 2019